Blue Plums & Weeds

By the same author of
Reaching Back for the Neverendings (1993)

BLUE

PLUMS

&

WEEDS

Poems

MARIO RENÉ PADILLA

PSPOETS
Los Angeles

All rights reserved under International and Pan-American
Copyright Conventions. Published in the U.S. by pspoets
Chase Maser, Editor in Chief
3120 4th St.
Santa Monica, CA 9 0405
pspoets@gmail.com

Printed in the United States of America
Cover Design and Original Art Work by Francesca Padilla
Layout Design by Chase Maser
FIRST EDITION

The author wishes to acknowledge the editors of the following publications
in which the following poems in this volume first appeared:
   The North American Review: "Once, I Wanted to be Ritchie Valens"
   Alligator Juniper: "Piled Boulders"
   The Ledge: "Frankenstein's Childhood Friend"
   TulipTree Review: "Mallarmé's Faune"
   Americas Review: "Keep the Grass Green Where He Lay" &
                   "*Veteranos* Day Parade"
   Explorations UP Alaska 1ˢᵗ prize: "Song of the Renegade Horses"
   Chiron Review: "My Cousin Charles"
   Writer's Digest: "*Veteranos* Day Parade" 4th place in Rhyming Contest

The collection *Blue Plums & Weeds* was also selected as a finalist in the
following national contests for book publication:
   Ohio University Press's 2015 Hollis Summers Poetry Prize
   Akron Poetry Prize 2008 (Rita Dove, judge)
   Snake Nation Press Poetry Prize (2007)

ISBN 978-0-578-81571-8

Contents

Without family,
poetry is candor without empathy, sunlight behind clouds.
For Christine, Francesca, Luciano, Miguel, Jake, Marcello,
Trevor, Laura, Gabriella, Nico, Marlo, and Armida

Blue Plums & Weeds

You see those piles of boulders that retain
The solemn motion of the rutting countryside,
Divide the ripening wheat from yellow lanes,
Support blue plums in trees the sun has dried . . .

Arthur Rimbaud

All the idle weeds that grow
In our sustaining corn.

Shakespeare

Good things lost among a wilderness of weeds.
Yet . . . evidence of a healthy soil.

Emily Brontë

I.

Blue Plums

Sitting in the Napoleon armchair, feet up
knees tucked tight against your chest, coffee cup
sipping, leafing the book you just took from my shelf
so beautiful at the breakfast table, like a Raphael
or an undressed wound, your breasts in nothing more
than the t-shirt I'd removed an hour or so ago
pursuing something silence said, flakes of croissant
on your chin, you say, "Tell me the truth."
I glance up, "Okay, newspaper says rain today . . . really."
The dark clouds in the skylight agree.

You sigh, lower your eyes
disturbed, fingering my dog-ear'd pages
highlights of Camus's meaningless debate
on the meaninglessness of meaning, absurd human state
swallowing his postulations as if they were parables
all the foibles of mortal life in the mind's inevitable hunt
to live long, feel pleasure, and just not hurt.

Smiling, I know full well where your head is heading.
I get up, switch the music from Beethoven to Miles
to better score the heaviness of your sighs
sad jazz eyes, *Kind of Blue* in green, tracking flies
tempted by my buttered toast dripping honey on sliced Brie.
"Now what truth would you ask of me that, breathing—
you don't already know?"

Hungry flies buzzing at the honey, gather in congress

to unite us. You smash one before it can react
"See!" I say. "Now there's the truth you seek
all in that one impulsive act." Camus was right
his answer to the essential question—
everything ends in our annihilation.
Both Camus and Miles are dead, as is Beethoven
and the cell phone you threw at my head
that hated number on the screen you know by heart
having disrupted our intimate morning in bed.
"So it seems," you whisper, "you don't love me then,"
your sad alluvium eyes wailing like a sax.
"Loving you has been a waste of time."

How can I explain, strangers that we are
we can hurt or not hurt, make love or not love
break things in anger or just sit together in peace—
with such limited time, who has time to waste?
Steeling ourselves against the clock
to face the disintegration in the mirror of our grieving
searching frantically at the end for the outline of soul
the fox hole, you know, *ghost guessed*
that gives life meaning somehow.
"Yes," I confess, "where you sit, she once sat,
leafing that same book you just took from my shelf.
So what?"

Raindrops on the skylight glass—end of drought
we should go out and celebrate the event, run in the rain
get wet, return invigorated and listen to the horn
singing its sharps and flats of a life once dreamt about
or you could smash another fly against the book
to remind us that we, at least, are still breathing.
Better yet, let's take ourselves back to bed
soaked in springtime's stubborn insistence on meaning
the main aim being, really   the killing of time
in the hunting and gathering of a mate.

Outside, there's a blue plum that rarely gives fruit
green buds form, then fall each summer
yellow from the plant
and once again they are there
stubborn little growths on wet boughs
dozens of babbling buds harping green their legitimacy
more buds, in fact, than have ever bloomed
and if they do?
First, they must survive pestilence and drought
then, hungry possums—
        death squads of a god we've never seen.

Mallarmé's Faune

for Karine

In a late afternoon dream, we are there still
lying naked beside a forbidden pond
having trespassed Le Comte's private preserve near Angers
slumbering in a symbolist's sun, interwoven legs and arms
our bodies warm, spun into a web of rising heat and sweat
pagan and young, like Mallarmé's *faune*
among willow fronds, wild bees, honeysuckle, and ants.

Waking now to the sound of rumbling California surf
the dream sits heavy on my chest
remembering your body in sunlight and sweat
your gothic gargoyles glaring down
from your favorite gabled-stone cathedral in Dijon
where you took me to see their squat ugly bodies
in chiseled rows, their grotesque masks of avarice and lust
the evils, you quipped, that tempt us whenever we're apart.

Some dreams are so resilient
we question at the vague awakening moment
the authenticity of the concrete world
the crashing California surf
the reasons I left France.
But in this afternoon's dream we are there still
lying naked and unsafe in water weeds at pond's edge
your gargoyles in the sun glancing down
their wicked stare I can't escape, shaded by my hand
you kept pressed against your breasts as we slept.

Suddenly, you whispered, "*Je t'aime*"
and their stone sardonic faces grimaced into frown.
They knew my knowledge of the French was limited
that in France, love is not an act of play but a gravity
a grave into which lovers submit themselves for burial.
The Plato of your perfect smile anticipated *Je t'aime aussi.*
Instead, I kissed your neck
the fleshy act of humans in a house of spirit.

So, hand in hand, we waded into the murky water
toes sinking into mushmeal sludge
lifted ourselves into a moss covered boat molding of disuse
oarless, rudderless, unnamed, like Rimbaud's *drunken boat.*
It held our weight as you lowered yourself upon me
and we sank into each other, panting and thrusting
the boat drifting in circles across the rippling, agitated water.

Ah! Those bottom planks
will never leave the contours of my back
your cry of pleasure on the mast haunts me still
the French sun, the pond, your gargoyles glancing down
the unnamed boat, our drifting lascivious pleasure
secluded by luciferous blossoms of dense vegetation
like those, I suppose, God planted in Eden.

Even now, safe-harbored in the Americas
through every monotonous suffocating summer since my return
lying in board shorts under palm trees and umbrellas

among crowds of sunbathers, the smell of sunscreen lotion
I dream of you, our naked bodies in that brown murky pond
the gargoyles you loved glancing down in the sun.

And in every version, the dream remains the same—
we wade into a forbidden pond, mythical and young
toes sinking into mushmeal sludge
toward a boat (still rotting there perhaps)
tucked among water weeds, moss laden, hidden
where, in each *reverie*, we enter and roll into each other
my back against the hull, your gargoyles glancing down
drifting in circles under Mallarmé's afternoon sun
your breasts, moist and firm against my chest
two pagan bodies slipping away unsafe—
into a grave in France.

Once I Wanted to Be Ritchie Valens

When I was ten, I wanted to be Ritchie Valens
brown skin like his, standing on a couch
I stood upon a stage in his burgundy shark's skin suit
a triple pick-up Fender strapped around my neck
(really just a broom and a piece of rope)
no soy marinero but a rock and roll star
that some blond blue-eyed girl from Germantown, Ohio
might finally find something in me to admire.

At twenty-one, I moved to Hollywood
and after a time, I wanted to be Cheech Marin.
It was the seventies and to be like him
I smoked reefer and said *órale* and *vato*
and *pinche cabrón ese.*
Then I went to Tijuana for one long day of drink and fun
with office friends named Matt, Allen and Fred
looking for cheap leather coats and some wrought-iron chairs
we drank cold beer in dark illicit bars
and I bought a ceramic bull with leather horns tipped in red
passing up a painting of Pancho Villa on black velvet
for a pair of maracas that said *Welcome to Tijuana.*
And crossing back into San Diego
they singled me out, ignoring the others in the car:
"Are you an American?" they asked
and how dare they ask me this in Spanish, me
with only three months of Cheech and Chong under my belt
and the high school Spanish I'd always flunked
and shit, wasn't I the same mid-western kid

they let pass that morning
without a single suspicious comment?

Then one day in the early eighties
I wanted to be Cesar Chavez.
I marched to stop the sale of grapes
wore a *serape* and a straw hat—even when it was hot.
You see, I'd fallen in love with Celia from Cal State
who took me to MEChA parties
where we drank Coronas with lime
while the room argued *politica* in impassioned tones of pride
and it was the first time I pronounced the *lls* of my name
like an *i* and an *a*
as I learned about my father's home town
I'd never heard about until that day.
At night we made love to Los Lobos and Santana
and she took me to meet her immigrant parents
translating everything I tried to say.

So I learned about Independence from Spain
that it wasn't celebrated on the fifth of May
and I took her to eat at Olvera Street
as she swallowed and smiled what she didn't want to say.
Till one day she informed me we'd never meet again
that I would never understand
what *la raza,* for her, had truly come to mean.
I bent my head and quietly said, "*Lo siento mi amor,*
but we are only what we learn to be."

Today, in poor but acceptable Spanish
I speak of Aztecs and Mayans—their ruins I've explored.
I can pronounce Nezahualcoyotl
and speak of the merits of education in bilingual
crusading for the deleted affirmative action
which gave me access to Paz's solitude inside a labyrinth.
Traveling the land of Fuentes, I crossed burning plains of Rulfo
through Soto's Chicano chapbooks
to Valdez's zoot suit *pachucos*
and I know where to find the best *nopalitos*—
and for the record I never check Hispanic
I answer to Latino.

And though I can never be an immigrant
I can be *la raza's* perpetual student
one single fist in the long embittered struggle
of Celia and all her kin
because in my own brown skin
I'm no less a Mexican kid
than the one who sang his way into Latino heaven
after they changed his name to Ritchie Valens
from Ricardo Esteban Valenzuela.

My Cousin Charles

She sat in a museum
twisting new heels around a size 10
playing with the bread knife   no
staring   thinking back on how she was
my cousin Charles who was now a woman.
We had chosen to meet at the museum
because it simply seemed appropriate
he being recreated and all
and she being the only male cousin
who shared my passion for abstract art.

I couldn't enter at first.
I peeked into the Gallery café
looking for that familiar head of hair
more apprehensive of the figures on benches
than the flock of fallen angels on the west wall.
And that he was "never allowed to get dirty"
kept surfacing like Styrofoam
on the liquid channel of memory.

Not noticing anyone I'd ever hugged
I turned to move into the next room
but a profile stayed imprinted
like the shape of light behind closed eyelids.
I had not seen him since he turned sixteen
the year he suddenly disappeared
and I was still searching for pimpled skin
with black horn-rimmed glasses.

I watched as she lit a cigarette
two mounds on her chest
twisting the Italian *cornetto* around her neck
which grandpa had given all us boys
for love and good fortune—
my tough Italian cousins from the south end.

And the angels on the wall began to scream
or was it my memories falling out of heaven
as something at that moment moved in me
from the beginning towards its end.
I felt the desire to turn and keep going
but when I looked she was still there
my cousin Charles now a woman
rummaging through her purse for another cigarette
glancing earnestly towards the door for someone
who might still remember having loved him.

But it had been twelve years and I was altered too.
My cousins had kept me somewhat informed
(though it was hard for them to say homosexual)
family events since my move to California
the different stages of his transformation
the search for love in gay bars, the beatings
reports of arrests by a cousin who is a policeman
my uncle who disowned him
my aunt, his *mother,* refusing to see him
but no one in the family ever said transvestite

he was "queer" that's all.
Things didn't get that strange
until the Christmas he showed up at gramma's
wearing a wig and a lavender dress.
God, I would give anything to have been there
in that basement when he walked down the stairs.
"It almost killed your grampa," my mother wrote
when she informed me of the operation—
and they think they know what balls are
my tough Italian cousins from the south end.

With a cultivated touch
she placed the lighter back into her purse
and looking up
saw me standing at the entrance and smiled.
And as I made a slow and deliberate approach
all I really wanted was to close my eyes
and remember that summer I taught him
how to swear and throw *bocce* balls
but the softness in his voice threw out "bitch"
like Marilyn Monroe
tossing out the first pitch for the Yankees.
There was something fatal even then in his voice.
He sang with a beautiful falsetto, and every Christmas
when we played Nativity at the family dinner
we always made him the angel.
Everything stopped when he sang "Silent Night"
in that sad and haunting tone.

It freezes my brain to see her sitting there
and hugging him longer than I would have
I remembered the story of the Italian castrati
who as children gave up human love
to sing for God.

On the Island of Lost Boys

The coastline of Cozumel, aqua swells
fishing boat masts tilt and sway
white gulls lilt on the rhythm of wind
and in the sun salty air, two boys run naked and pure
playing on the abandoned shore.
They have found a conch shell
extricated from the shell-white sand
their treasure chest of precious stones
driftwood, sea weed, and tumbled glass.

I swing lazy in a rope woven hammock
invisible observer of this distant theater
as each boy lifts the conch shell to his lips
blows on the tapered end, the sound of sea ships
and ancient rite filters through the cerulean air.
How simple the sound, how powerful the note.
If only the poet could get to it this way
sound the note, spot it hidden in the brain
buried in passages of utilitarian words
sounding through disquieting times
echoing the mysterious rumbling of the sea
the deep psychology of the human spirit—
the simple sense of having something to say
raising it to the lips and saying it.

I come here winters to worship time, the hypnotic surf
the sound nothing-to-do makes under sunshine and palms
to find two spirits running wild and free

children once sacrificed to Ixchel on this Isle of Swallows
barter for the gods, more rain and better crops
long before Cortés brought cannons and smallpox
or Cantinflas margaritas and chips to poolside bars
in glass-stacked hotels standing tall and obscene
sprouting like corn stalks in fashionable Cancun.

I capture their play, soon to be eternal children
facing out to greet me from these pages
the conch shell forever to their lips
sounding the rich tone of azure Caribbean
calling 1,000-year-old sea turtles to come lay their young
two little Mayan gods roaming Ah-Cuzamil-Peten
forever blowing their conch shell melody to the sun
like the bride and groom on Keats's Grecian urn—
who forever will remain in love, inconsummate.

In concrete L.A.
I live out my plans in traffic jams of tedious ambition and lust
crammed bodies on the stalled 405, sucking dioxide in the heat
though at times, sitting behind the wheel
I open this journal
to hear two children, brown and eternal
    for ever panting, and for ever young
blowing a conch shell they found buried in the sand.

Frankenstein's Childhood Friend

for Jimmy

My chubby childhood friend and I decided to make a film
inside the lens of my parent's super eight
the first one of its kind in our part of town
he became the monster come to terrorize the place
in the bedroom lab where I created secret friends.
But he was the flesh n' bone kind
and all I needed to know of him—I knew:
the teacher he disliked at school
his favorite ride at the summer fair
the monkey he'd mimic at the county zoo
the same ugly shoes he always wore
the days he could play and the day for chores
and always I knew the cinnamon rolls he'd choose
standing at the curb in early morning light
waiting for the bread truck to make its daily tour.

He was the body that replaced silence
and on the short walk home from school
we talked of nothing we would one day know
like desires, loss, or the countries we might go
nor what he thought of time and love
the pain one day we'd be powerless to subdue
the father he adored, the mother he hardly knew
or birth control, ecology, the plight of the poor
and never a concern about unjust war
all of this as distant as the non-existence of God.
He was Frankenstein's monster, that's all
my overweight convenient friend

who was never allowed any innuendo of a crush.
I didn't even know what sex he'd choose
if choosing then was a choice at all.
When I moved away, so did time and friendship
to a new world drawn to proximate state lines
no longer linked by needs conveniently matched
confidences shared in flash-lit tents
over potato chips consumed in the exchange of comics
never knowing how the other truly felt.

Once in an isolated moment of nostalgia I looked him up
a rare trip home, a sentimental journey never before allowed
and after talk of the cushioned days of school
the giggling we could never stop
the army we formed in his greasy garage
(he the captain, but I the general)
some light exchanges, notes on raising boys
the struggling of his firm
there was little left of memory for us to lose.
So we spoke of our long-lost film I wanted to restore
laughed aloud as he growled, "alone, bad . . . friend, good."
In the evening darkness I left him with a hug
something as young friends we could never do.

When I heard he died at 45
a body so heavy with chore and pain of sewing up
I sent his sons each a copy of the tape
so that they might know their father from the man
in the whole damn scheme of growing up.

The Succulent Taste of Plums

There's nothing so sensuous as the succulent taste of plums
messy in the mouth, soft yellow pulp in blue-purple skins
delicious sloppy-drippings over fingers, hands, and tongue
like when Carlos Williams told her he had stolen them.

My neighbor likes apples, sliced thin, peeled clean
so neat and quartered intact, de-cored, green
fruit with no real bother save a thumb that can bleed
one slip in slicing skin removing those annoying seeds.

I see him carting bushels to his proud cellar of waste
others on the ground the difference and disparate in our taste
I savor plums one by one, stained in blue juice dripping
his apples in baskets, decorative, discolored, drying.

In summer, each plum I pick precious from the bough
handled like royalty, I mourn the unripened buds that fall
to pestilence and leaf curl fungus, nature's relentless blight
as such, God says value less, better verse than tedious plot.

Even so, at times, I envy his apple blossoms' promise
Why not? another stellar year, his cellar heaped in produce
like the bushels of words he piles in novels so abundant
multiplying in baskets, like loaves and fishes—so redundant.

The result—apple pie, so popular on the American table
poets know the plummer's fate each visit to Barnes and Noble.
Still, I harvest plums, the budding precious few
sloppy dripping, stain disturbing, so ripe-juicy and blue.

Pine Tree Fortress

As a boy I found them
Christmas trees discarded in icy alleys
lying naked and obscene in snow banks
or stuffed in containers for refuse collection.
To an empty lot I dragged them
piled atop my red-rusted wagon
to build myself a pine tree fortress.

Layered over a deep shoveled hole in the snow
I crawled inside, cold and joyously hidden
breathing in the holiday season
pine scent still seeping from the wood
silver tinsel clinging to dry needles
solitary tenant of my imaginary world
where I prayed no trouble could find its way in—
my parent's heated arguments, schoolyard fists
the lunchroom confrontations of every biracial kid
hunkered down in white Ohio with less-than-white-skin.

Up and down the alleys I found them
abandoned icons of harmony and peace
their melancholy branches stripped of ornament.
I lugged them to my secret fortress
to crawl inside and pass the hours
with my other less-than-fortunate friends:
Copperfield, Twist, the irascible Finn
holding out to the very end—the circled date
on the kitchen calendar when school would start again.

"One day," I'd say, "I'll show `em—
every last one of `em"—this was certain.
I dreamt of things they couldn't possibly envision
inside the theater of my boundless imagination
wild fantasies bred in a broken tossed-out folding chair
victories won, bullies vanquished
beneath the pain of my surface reality
hidden away from their menacing glares
white freckled noses and racial slurs
cushioned warm in my wool-heavy coat
wombed inside my pine-scented fortress—
as I must have felt, once, in the belly of my birth
far from the surface of the frozen earth.

Piled Boulders

for Armida

Driving across the high desert
the great expanse prays like a devout Catholic.
I think of you, pull off, straddle now a rock
where a lizard slithered away, rock heat, no water
only desert brush and sun
and you fill the burnt shadows the piled boulders make
in the lonesome stretch of heat and sand.

I imagine our childhood God a timekeeper
pacing the rise and fall of our daily laps.
In Catholic school uniforms we were taught
humans are born into original sin—a shared destiny
shame in the groin for some ancient crime
that wanting to know more beyond God's will
beyond the simple trek toward salvation is a sin
a curse upon us all, the whole Eve and serpent thing.

But somehow, on contrary course, we grew up—
mother managing our progressive faces on the fridge.
"So as not to lose track of time," she said
capturing us as well on super eight smiling into the lens
unfettered smiles in audioless silence.
Only now, the click and shutter of the old projector
in an age of tape disturbs the projection of our innocent faces
freeze-framed on your last unencumbered smile, then mine
before sex and marriage, death and divorce
our unsuspected destinies yet to transpire—
when you would never be *her* again and I no longer *him*.

I see the sun bank into the sand and realize
it has suddenly turned cold.

You write that you are dreaming of him again
the son angels spirited away
begging God's mercy to stroke away his gash
like Mary at the foot of the cross.
His presence still among the furniture you say
in the kitchen plates, the séance at the table failed again
his faint image dispersed by morning light
in cigarette smoke trailing up, tobacco into ash
taking stale bread, like a bird, with coffee and rum
in ragged slippers, waiting out the curse of dawn
another day's waste of time's rise and fall
that does not flow, as some insist, like a river—
one uninterrupted current to the sea.

No, we advance like mice in the great experimenter's maze
lapping the wheel, we channel along
then skitter into the chute, blocked at the edge of escape
we turn, go into another, stop, turn
keep on advancing through the labyrinth of instinct
until one day we reach these boulders
piled like grey clouds, climb and straddle
then watch the sun sink pink into the sand
exhausted by the legacy of original sin.

I still pray sometimes but don't know why

here, before descending back into the city
for *him,* who died in cauterizing life
for *her,* who died beneath a son's unbroken fall
and always, for the failure of human love.
And not yet ready to return to slotted, air-conditioned life
I pray to time, before the memory of having lived it
sitting cross-legged on a desert rock   to just start walking.
Perhaps out there, in quiet rendezvous between earth and sun
no grief exists, no time
where everything, at once, is taken and returned.

Another Midnight Promenade

The city center is empty tonight
street musicians all played out
and I walk an angry route
on the chilly street-lamped Promenade.
Collar turned up, both hands in pockets
my mind wanders back to a military school in the south
turrets on medieval battlements, before civil rights
nestled in the foothills of Georgia's Blue Ridge mountains.
I can still hear *taps*, its haunting bugle notes in the dark
lying in the secluded barrack, fearing after lights out
the older boys in starched gray collars and cuffs
who couldn't abide the color brown
in their uniformed platoon of confederate white.

Walking against the current, my cold hands ache
they bear scars from dormitory walls angry fists make
like jackhammers, cracking cement
breaking apart my innocence—learning so young how to hate.
All the battering hard fought lessons suffered long ago
in those bunk-bedded barracks, penned up with their drawl
rattling my invisible fetters anchored to cinder block walls
pushed down, bleeding on the spotless red-oil'd floor
I'd recently mopped `cause the oldest ordered me so
rising up with rage to stage yet another impotent defense.
All those tearful *Lord of the Flies* kind of nights when
uncontrollable boy-men surrounded the smallest of the dark.
How the Angelus rained down like silver water then.

But no one dare tell what seen, what blows heard—
in truth, their fists less damaging than their hurtful words.
So with growing muscle and temper I learned how to fight
never thoughtful reason—reason could never block a right.
What reason then with good ol' boys just learning how to shave
thin hairs from pimpled, pockmarked skin.
Part of my heart is buried there still
in Georgia's red-clay confederate earth
wrapped in a spotted cloth, the cartridge ink I spilled
on every letter home, begging for safe passage north.

Tonight, after all the years, anger still corrupts the brain
its curse buried deep inside my legacy of hate—
all the Skips, Butches and Jim-bobs of the world
terrorizing a child's time, usurped by their redneck quips
disparaging words I continue to lug about
like a shoulder harness attached to an ox
or a cross I bear up a hill, head slumped
ploughing the Promenade on a cold crucifying night
making my way back home to you
after yet another horrible midnight fight.

I think of how I left you sobbing in the sheets
huddled miserable in the vacuum of our vicious words
yet another fallout, the verbal bombing of the self
the alcohol you consume to caress your own troubled past
pain attracts pain I guess—a mutual need to save what's left.

I slink into the yard like the night prowling possum
that's been pillaging the precious plums on the bough
step toward the unlit porch and gently knock
wait penitently by the door you'll eventually unlock
to fall into the fold of each other's arms and weep
whispering, "It's alright, it's alright. I understand"
heading for the disheveled bed—
harbor of our momentary compromise.

If Only I Could Be Bar Stool Bukowski

I wish I could drink like *barfly* Bukowski
puking out his truth on a barroom floor
sweet oblivion in the brain
poetry for the dispossessed, the insane.
Glass for glass in my bar stool recitation
I'd deliver clever diatribes on the limitations of verse
mi alma y mi corazon thrown in for cultural reference
explore the damage of love's inevitable curse
or why the earth, one day, will smash into the sun
all in exchange for drinks or a blow job in the john
while Coltrane on the jukebox saxophones the room—
oh, how I wish I could drink like him and just stay numb.

But mine is too weak a stomach for drink
my greatest weakness—my instinct for life
an all-consuming ambition to multiply and survive—
hell, I don't drink 'cause I'm afraid to die.
Aside from that, I look ridiculous on a stool
hovering in space with no levers of self-control.
I met a girl there once, who loved her drink
mistook me for the *barfly* poet (whom she loved to quote)
till she found me out—"You're no Charles by a long shot."
And she was right!

No, I'm just a pedestrian mouthing metaphors on a stool
holding my center of gravity, trying not to fall
who must be watched, rushed to the bathroom to puke
a sucker vulnerable to regulars tapping him for drinks.

Now my father had it down, the bar stool life
though he revealed in certain sober times
how on dark nights he drank tunnels into alone.
"Drinks son are nobody's friend
till you reach the *blacksipped* end."
Still, I ponder sometimes how it's done
sitting in a bar on a high wooden stool
but not Charles' grungy dives,
sweaty whores and drugs in stalls
more like the friendly bar in *Cheers*
where drinking seems a happy choice
a joke enticing juice for camaraderie and fun.
Oh God, how I envy him.

How I wish I could be bar stool Bukowski
rocket into orbit, scribe the famous face of God
hold court with my verse from a bar stool pulpit
blame sobriety for the misery of my self-inflicted wounds
not my pitiful self, all my failed attempts at love.
Yes, if only I could drink like *barfly* Bukowski—
I'd sit on a stool and just be numb.

Keep the Grass Green Where He Lay

por mis abuelos de S.F. del Rincon, Guanajuato

Cuando veníamos al Norte, I came with hope
and what you ask me here
tears into my heart like a bullet.
Is there anything special I want to say on it?
Of course there is. But I couldn't say it all
for what is all would not fit, though we would pay
what little we have for more words, as once we did
the *coyote,* searching for a better way in.

I remember when we crossed Tijuana to San Ysidro, I said,
"*Mira mijo,* we're here, isn't it beautiful?" "*Sí* Mama,"
Joselito said with eyes on the dark green grass. He lay in it
rolled in it, and said, "it's softer than my bed."
The tall buildings of San Diego with fountains of water
the bay with sailboats, everywhere dark green grass
sprinklers on the beautiful lawns, water pipes in the fields
water everywhere, even to clean the streets.
Oh! It was wonderful!

In our *puebla* we had a hard, dry life.
There were eight of us. We lived in a two-room
wooden shack with a straw roof and dirt floors.
There was little rain. The closest drinking water, a well
some distance away. No electricity, I cooked on log fires
and washed clothes on rocks at a dribbling stream.
But here we have an apartment, a little rundown, yes
but with electricity. Though the furniture is secondhand
we have running water. The landlord leaves us alone.

He says fumigation is too expensive
and the water heater has been broken too long now
but Joselito never complained.

On the ranch near our village
his older brothers washed in the stream, they left
school and worked hard, though *papi* sat with them evenings
to teach them what he knew. But here, Joselito grew to know
how the frogs he once chased wild in the fields
looked on the inside. He kept his numbers so neat
and learned how to read the English words. I don't know
exactly when he began talk of quitting school.
He wanted money to buy a car and new clothes. "I'll cut
grass with papa," he said. Then the problems started.
He hid things. They cut tattoos into his skin
and when his eyes were thin, said things to me
that without God I could never forgive. I'd say,
"Go to your new family, you don't need us."
But for two years every Sunday we paid him visits
two hours we drove, and brought tortillas and tamales
and what personal things the guards would let in.

You see, don't ask me what to say on it
all that I carry in my heart would not fit.
I gave him his own key when he returned
but he was closed so tight
always looking through the window
like some terrible animal keeping watch. That last night

with such a strange look in his eyes, he said quietly,
"I remember the old field, papa cutting into dry dirt
and you saying before we left, 'If only there were water
you don't suffer where there is water.
Things go well for your whole life.'"
Then he walked to the sink, like in a dream
turned the faucet on, let it run, smiled at me, and left.

And I can only wonder now if those boys who passed
in the low black car, really knew what he could have been.
Sí. I know, forgive me, you are busy. How much for
In Memory Of? Oh . . . then
just place the name and date like this
and keep the grass green where he lay.

Song of the Renegade Horses

I remember at sunset
sand swirling in the chaos of hooves, how we
sent the horses galloping across the rose-painted desert.
Then at night, singing before the fire
how you sat cross-legged on an indigenous shawl
interwoven with a polished pointed bone and loom
into the colors of the wild horses we men had run
hot and lathered into the log-notched stall
the work that made us men somehow
as you methodically stirred a corn and comino broth—
your delicate throat filling our mute observation with song.

They were not songs to identify story, but rare sounds
like when the trees bend and moan, leaning in the Westers
blowing steel cold air off the snowcapped Sierras.
And after the firesong and warm broth
with coyotes howling their own dark cavernous craving
I remember your coarse hands on the nape of my neck
the nimble fingers that spun the fabric we lay upon
that weaved the multi-colored shawl as you sang
braided hemp rope used to capture the foals
my brown skin now the *masa* you worked, kneading flesh
your powerful fingers lifting off the day's labor of pain.

And I remember after sex the space inside our hut
before we drifted off to sleep
that at times seemed filled with the sound of hooves
the young dreams you rode at seventeen, wild-eyed

stampeding through the meditative hush
after sex and satiation's solitude.
When you came to me at twenty, you had already learned
how to sing their departure, your passionate untamed dreams
shifting and lunging disquietly on the pillow
straining against the rope tethers like renegade horses—
how you planned to sing yourself out of the desert.

And I remember the mature round belly you carried
with the lonesome task of singing.
You died together on the bloody shawl
in the crude and suffocating landscape.
And always, I'll remember the sound of your final song
that climbed up out of your empty womb
and through the uneasy horses
till it tore a hole through the log-notched fences
sending whatever you once believed of music—
wild and waterless—out into the unforgiving desert.

Descent into a Heartland State

Flying down into a heartland state
having left a city in the arid west—
my adopted concrete desert of cars—
I see through the oval glass from an airplane vantage
trees of dense multicolored forests
their red-russet leaves and massive trunks
that appear like a theater scrim
the landscape of my autumn's childhood.
A fabulous river next, where I once fished
but the trees first. I'd forgotten how they look
too long away, the red maples and mighty white oaks.
How I loved watching their leaves drop
floating fatal to the ground.

Seen from the sky, the trees seem planted by design
arranged rows of enjambed twigs, unnatural borders
separating furrowed fields from rye-weed grass pastures
acres upon acres stitched together, like a handmade quilt
a tapestry of farms and freshly plowed earth
as if the county's 4H met and chose the course
each farmer's plow and tractor must take—
some humans like their lives patterned and stitched
a planned and ordered design within which to exist.

My forehead pressed against the glass
absorbed in the landscape spread out before me
I watch as we descend into John Glenn's airport
my disordered chaotic life left momentarily behind

And once again, I can't help but think in Camus' thoughts
a stranger here too since birth: *with what intensity*
nature negates human dominion on earth.
The trees remain—Camus' fractured skull like Yorick's
does not.

The trees persist, unlike humans
who live in such haste and die so quick
sleepless, stressed, ravenous, depressed
overprescribed, overfed, unfulfilled, lost
till their battered bodies simply give out, or worse
found in cars wrapped around a pole, Camus style—
crumpled and destroyed by intemperate life
or massacred like cattle in some stupid war.

But these superior trees, patient and thick
continue their slow, steady pattern of growth
deeply rooted in season after season of leaf-meal mulch
inner circles that mark their tenancy on earth
the oldest, I understand, eleven centuries in Greece.
And descending slowly into my heartland state
I see the trees first, thick trunks tall and erect
the river next, but the trees first, and smile   knowing
not all of nature's inhabitants are without progress—
the crude process, coarse and indifferent, still works.

II.

Weeds

Perhaps it's too much trouble, I don't know—tilling idle weeds,
preparing the garden ground for next spring's harvest.
Summer's production gone—once so proud in the planting
just a sweaty chore now, dirt-tired, thirst-slaking labor
gripping calloused handles, backbone sore.
I lie down, depleted, exhausted
somewhere between industry and the impulse to sleep
a tear at the edge of a lash.

Removing the disheveled look of death requires purpose.
I look at this unsightly plot and think
let the weeds have their day, spread their indigenous crop
more natural anyway, the look of chaos, wild and effortless.
For what's the point of sowing? If memory serves correct
working the ground for seeding produced small corn last year
chard tough and chewy, rotten zucchini, and green peppers
well, they decided not to show up at all
though the tomatoes were good (the ones without worm holes)
better produce on grocery store shelves.

I lie down in savàsana, torso like a corpse, face up
to meditate on a drifting cloud, lazy in reverie
how close I came to death at birth, how it was I was produced
small and feeble. So anxious to take life's initial breath
I moved too much, wrapped that vital cord around my neck
till doctors cut and yanked me out.
They thought the blue baby dead, my mother recalls
instead, I thrashed and cried my will to live.

But I'm exhausted by nature's jousting match
persistent drought, incessant pests, leaf curl blight
all the dangerous forces I parry and riposte
that have tried for years to take my garden out.
I fear I have no strength left to fight
knowing full well, nature and I are not an even match
not even in the same weight class.
So this year, I'm inclined to let the soil rest, let the weeds rout
get up, drive my ass to the store, forget this tedious chore.
Why drain the precious hours I have left   right?

"Not a chance," the promise a patch of earth represents.
It drags me up, impossible to drop this goddamned handle
to not relive April's springtime idyll—
the annoying potential of all that life has to yield.
So I furrow the first row imagining the ideal
larger corn, arm-length zucchini,
maybe even some peppers this year
if not the biggest, juiciest tomatoes I've ever produced
always from the sweat of hope
knowing full well—
only seeds sown get the chance to live.

Attacking the Kalipaui Trail

for Maureen

In a sky-blue basket
the yellow breeze carries the sun.
The children, like sandpipers, run the day long
to and from the recurring surf
till their hair turns pink in the astonished twilight
the disappearing globe red as a cut pomegranate.

After dark, we ascend back into lush mountains
green over Maui, our campsite in the dank forest
ankle deep in mud from yet another evening's rain.
In our intimate tent (the children asleep in theirs)
my brown body rises in the pupils of your eyes
like the dolphin that magically appeared
dancing its curved back in the wake of our kayak.
You love me again, now that we've come to Hawaii
but when we swim hand in hand, snorkeling along the reef
you say I'm like the yellowtail sunfish
that flits enticingly close but cannot be reached.

So we've come here to find love's provisos again—
in the too-lazy heat, in the libidinous hot-white sand.
But four days out, I'm already tan-tired of the sun
the green screaming palm trees, purple restless fish
the irony of the strangling *lais* placed around our necks
as we deplaned, the burning in my salt-watered lungs
swimming aimless in the monotonous sea
or sipping fruity drinks, little umbrellas in a glass.

Feeling my discontent, you take charge and insist
"Collect the tents! Let's hike the Kalipaui Trail,"
infamous challenge of fortitude and will.
Attacking the dangerous crest that barely holds two feet
we bind together as we have always done
resolved to pull our children across the abyss
your strong legs leading the way. We tramp
seven miles eating mangos hanging plentiful from trees
until the sudden sound of a waterfall magnifies our thirst
spouting coolness from a tumbling pool
that dissolves the sticky mango juice and cools our burning hair.
With water cupped into your palms
you anoint my head, "Newly baptized," you say.
"We must forget the old, the reasons why we failed."

But last night, our naked shadows against the tent
no *body,* not even Rumi, could retrieve my contaminated heart
yearning like an addict for his ancestral lands
not this all-consuming ocean, fruity drinks and ukulele bands
but plaster saints in musty temple-stone cathedrals
that brood in the confluence of bloody Aztec foundations
ancianos who live at the foot of the Chichonal volcano
and stare one-eyed across cornfields, sipping pulque
to better shape-shift into eagles
or kneel at a rack of a hundred flickering candles
before Tonatzin de Guadalupe in her rock grotto abbey.

Or further still

back to the land of my great grandfather's castles
to Falla's *Nana,* his coplas de flamenco sung in Granada
where Lorca, murdered, cried his pain in deep *cante hondo*
as weathered-face gypsies strum their guitars
growling out their *siguiriyas* in toothless deep-throated passion
the *duende* pounding his heels to the soul's rhythmic clapping.

Forgive me love, as much as I love you
your yellow sun over six islands cannot keep me.
I'm exhausted by the perfect blue, your cheerful *diario* blue
the reason why we failed blue, the safety in being yours blue—
like Odysseus, fools must heed the Siren's when they sing.
Tonight, I sleep with *huaraches* strapped to my feet
and dream myself ascending the Pyramid of the Sun
balancing a feathered headdress of Quetzal plumes.

Or further still
to the Moorish courtyard of the Alhambra,
pounding my heels, in cadence, clapping
twirling myself into a state of madness
as the *cantaor flamenco* strums his bleeding guitar.

Vacant House in Venice

for Marcel Rafael (1981-83)

I hear him moving about the house after dusk
in the outline of candle shadow and dust
wandering the empty recovered rooms
his inaudible crying rises like a haunting Gregorian chant.
At night, I sit in somber meditation on the hardwood floor
below a stained glass window, incense trailing up
mea culpa, mea culpa, like a Franciscan monk
in my hooded brown robe—a deep mantra rising
a chant of remorse, in my solitary conference with the dark.

At dawn, I rise to greet him. Taking his hand
we commiserate with the backyard sparrows
near the swing we hung when he was born.
It hangs there still on rust-frozen swivels
corrupted by disuse, a broken swaying in the rain under the pine.
And again I'm forced to consider the weed-corrupted garden
where we once knelt in Gromulch and newly-wedded bliss
clawing out dead roots, rocks, and shards of glass—
proud to plant in our newly purchased house
all our future in the making.

Vacant now, the house no longer echoes life—
bouncing balls, broken plates, piano sessions
songs written to commemorate the second coming.
He leads me now with his ghostly hand
to the wooden swing, smiles from the swaying sensation
as I pace lamentation on the moss-covered bricks.
Had you suspicions then, that one day I'd return

like to the dog-eared pages of a much read book
to harvest the blue plums hanging from the bough
not wasted in their splashed and grounded sadness.

A more dependable life is what you wanted.
Of course, who wouldn't want a more solid ground
though I left myself alone to savor the details:
plum cake cooling on the kitchen table
fig bars baking in the O'Keefe & Merritt
fresh tomatoes and basil from our plentiful garden
our eldest loping across the yard, her own fairyland kingdom
till her brother arrived and made us four—
our abundant life stretched out before us
like a long vanishing road.

I found a key rusting in the Bougainvillea
door locks changed, it's useless to me now
so I wear it round my neck like a scapular
meditating on Saint Francis in the rampant weeds
his head broke off in transit—I've glued it back on.
And like the friar-painter Fra'Angelico on the river Po
I live now like a scribe, inventing verse
seeking purpose in chanting my soul-inspired words—
all my treasures forfeited for the hunger of art.

Dusk descends on Venice and sober night returns
where I've settled for a season of winters.
His little hand greets me again, outstretched

beckoning me toward the wooden swing.
And rest assured, I'll be the mother to him this time
cradle his burning fevers, arrest his debilitating seizures
that only your voice as he swung could calm—
your soothing song singing him to sleep.

In the mornings, I rise with the sparrows
shake the dampness of the grave off my blanket
as I peel myself from the wooden slats
red marks slashed across my back like a flogging
having spent the long night singing him to sleep
in the rusted, motionless swing.

Christmas Concert Tie

Pine scent at the open door, hesitating entrance
I peek into the festive room, fir tree in the familiar corner
trimmed red and green with our yuletide decorations.
Frozen at the threshold, like a fawn in headlights
motionless without a sound, simply watching her hands
garland the mantel, figure fuller now, still beautiful
her long, artistic fingers I've kissed and touched
weaving holly with the skill of a clockmaker.

Bolting for the car and evening's anonymity
away from the confluence of memory and misery
I turn the key, let the engine idle, hoping, son, you'll come out.
Running through the door, you shout, "Pop, wait!"
your white unbuttoned collar flapping like a pigeon
my borrowed shirt too big for your neck.
I step out into the lamplight to exchange hugs
as you buy my feeble explanation: "Have to rush out of town
son. A business trip that can't be postponed."
You look away (I think you knew).

"At least help me with my tie," you say.
You'd asked me to attend your Christmas concert recital.
"The whole family will be there," you casually announced.
"Even mom's new boyfriend will be there." Awkward,
the naive innocence of a child's unmalicious thoughts.
Like the cruelty of April—to see us all sitting together
flushed with pride over your performance.
"You have to tie my tie, 'cause Mom can't do it."

We laugh as I guide your fingers
long and delicate like your mother's. My thick hands
twist the fabric through repeated miscalculations.
And I wonder, who will teach you how to shave
slip the razor into your fingers or the hammer into your hands
to teach you how to nail
without nailing yourself against the wood?
Or better still, how to dance with a woman, when it's time.
How to hold her in your arms at day's end
waltz her around the room giggling and mumbling
sweet endearments.

How I wish I had danced with her
rushed through the door and kissed her full and true
not the obligatory touch-of-lips kind, always in a rush—
but Rodin's eternal kiss, intense, heartfelt
that love need never grow old.
I tie your tie in the headlights
interlace the loops as I have always done,
just as I learned watching my father's thick hands
twist a perfect Windsor before the broken mirror—
the night he left.

Along the South Downs Way

for Francesca

Winter in England, the rainy season
when twilight turns cold and comes earlier than expected.
Good to see the last rays pierce the persistent clouds
slivers of beams splaying, penitent, like a holy card benediction
illuminating patches of pastoral fields, meadows of sheep
in fields nocturnal, like perfectly placed piano chords by Chopin.
And with a determined hand, you pull me from my desk
point to the pink window and in your maturing voice exclaim,
"Papa, you'll never find words for this."
(instinctively, I know she's right)
So, I shut down the keyboard, inhale a silent hallelujah
and say, "Let's take a walk along the South Downs Way."

Grabbing coats, black rubber knee-high boots
Scarves and gloves, some woolen hats, we head out.
I've enough of searching insoluble words
just another pair of hooves among the bleating herd
grazing the same overgrazed leaves of grass, seeking tenure
while my own work suffers, languishing in a drawer.
And after all, it *is* your time—and our visits come too infrequent
that this one should grow dark unventured.

Twilight pastoral, we spot deer along the muddy trail
seven galloping doe, nose to rump
a young one tucked deep inside the fold
the buck seeking the way forward, proud.
You climb a wooden fence for a better view
I look at you and think, "My God, she already has breasts."

With your dancer's legs balanced on a post
you leap and pirouette to demonstrate
at thirteen, you're still my *piccolina ballerina*
though a space has opened between those who were us.

A proud young filly approaches, forcing us from her fence.
She bounces on hind hooves, blowing out steam
running wild about the small field that was all hers once
before rams and ewes came munching and bleating
following her about. "The night's grown cold," I say.
"Better head back. You've an early morning flight."

Passing manicured hedgerows, a full-rising moon
has teed itself up on a 400-year-old chimney.
Drifting smoke rises from the flue, ritual-like
as the burning of the dead among the Lakotas.
I'm losing the child in you, I think to myself
as we trudge hand in hand along the Way in mud-heavy boots,
our faces nestled deep in scarves and pulled-down hats
feeling all the emptiness of the day after Christmas.

We pass the filly again, her body calm now
though her eyes remain keen and alert
always vigilant for an exit.
And pulling you close in silence, I imagine
you'll never be this young again, so guileless and free—
soon to be contained inside your own teenage fence
boys in jeans, cool tattoos and needs

following you about in Doc Martins,
their cheesy lines at the lunchtime tables—
the galloping world of sex in all that high school drama.

Ah, my little *mummenschanz*, without knowing how or when
we all grow up—fleeing the field of innocence.
Youth doesn't last, the years clip by so fast, unnoticed.
I just pray, sooner than later, you will discover
the untamable woman inside of you, heart, skin and soul free
the breed you were meant to be
like all wild and elemental things
though who and what you were to me will drift away
a plume of black chimney smoke rising
disappearing into the atmosphere, ritual-like
        drifting away with old spirits.

Dreaming into Flight

I used to dream I could fly
the nightly sessions I'd anticipate.
I didn't hover like an eagle or levitate
flap my arms as a Neanderthal might
in his frantic attempt to escape a Sabertooth's bite.
No, my young flights were more theatric than scientific
they began with a run, then a coordinated leap
my legs, two springs that sprung me off the ground
and with extended arms, Superman style, fists clenched
for supersonic power—I penetrated the sky.

Most experts agree
not all children dream themselves into flight
but the ones who do hold high expectations of life.
Soaring in dreams means they'll reach the highest heights
succeed in whatever endeavor they attempt.
For young male flyers it's a simple act
An ambitious, energetic leap, a lifting-off from the earth
ungrounded at ten by two loaded balls
attached like anchors to the scrotum in the groin
unaware of what *cojones* were designed to do—
till their first ecstasy of emission, sudden semen on the spread
sends them crashing, head first, to the ground.

All male flyers with whom I speak
chatting over beers in mid-town bars
forever grounded after the fabulous *fall*
say, "Yeah, I used to fly all the time as a kid."

"You too?"
"Sure. Superman style, right?"
complain about women, and all that is about woman
good ones lost in their continual grazing
feet trudging through desire and muck
endlessly searching for yet another fuck
sadly admit those nightly flights came to a sudden halt
around the age fourteen.

My fourteen-year-old son is not speaking to me now
says I treat him immature.
He wants to stay out late with a girl he adores
but I just want to ease my Icarus down
his pimples exploding, new deeper voice, larger feet
thicker hair beneath the arms. He's a good kid
confused like all the rest because he just found out
in dreams, he can no longer rise off the ground.
"Lately," he says, "I can hardly run"
grazing the strange new wonderland
of Victoria's Secret lust
lingerie ads stuffed between the sheets.

Winter Visit to Massachusetts

for Marcello

Footprints in the snow, plowing up a steep hill
on my son's private Massachusetts school grounds
I struggle in winter's cold I'm no longer used to.
I was comfortable, reading poetry in the campus B & B
Sharon Olds with coffee—how *sex without love* is a
solitary selfish act. When looking out my frosty window
I saw a distant steeple, like a beacon, if not a solemn symbol
that teased me out of my warm linen sheets.
Time to pay God that long overdue visit—drawn by the
pilgrim's promise of an old stone chapel.

Reaching the door with shortened breath, pulling on the handles
I see I've been locked out—turned away at heaven's gate
punishment for chronic disbelief I guess.
Prayers never spoken—answers never granted.
The Floor Has Sunk, sign says. *Condemned, Stay Out!*
just a bunch of mortared stones with stained glass windows
its rotted wood corroded by the seasons.
But the bell tower at the hour still chimes eight o'clock
imagine that—keeping its regularity like ocean waves
or the vibrating tones of Ptolemy's music of the spheres
though God has split, locking the door on the way out.

But I refuse to abandon my climb's wages.
"Oh ye needy pilgrim," the old chapel whispers.
"My bells continue ringing…come hither my child"
its Pavlovian appeal slightly irritating in a British accent.
So stubbornly, I try the door on the far side

another entrance God might have forgotten. Locked as well.
But a fluttering in the eaves attracts my attention
a hungry sparrow warbling in its nest
the others, more capable of flight, already flown south
a broken wing, most likely, for by instinct it would fly
to escape a winter's death, to sing in warmer climes.
In a garden of snowy weeds Saint Francis stands his ground
palming a stone carved sparrow
as the bell tower rings the quarter hour, 8:15.
Seems even in the waning seasons
some things simply refuse to stop singing.

Sweeping the snow off of Francis' bench
I sit to meditate on my son's chosen path.
He sings tonight, the lead in the school's annual musical.
He'd asked if I would make the trip. "Of course," I said
and with a father's pride, I took the next flight out.
You see, I'm determined to be of some use in his life
(though I stopped singing in Hollywood long ago).
I can advise how to project to the back of the auditorium
methods for handling those opening-night jitters
nothing more to give than that   really.

Certainly, I can't share the experience of great success—in fact
I'd change his mind if I could—though he has the talent.
"Just here for him," I whisper to St. Francis
as the bell tower chimes the half-hour. Though I know
harsher days will follow this evening's applause

so addictive those standing ovations
like sex without the messiness of love.

Abandoning my vigil, I return across my backward tracks
ankle-deep in snow, ill-chosen shoes, toes soaked to the bone
to find my son's dorm. He's awake—hungry of course
shouting and rousting among roommates snapping towels.
How fortunate his mother's new husband can afford the fees
Uma Thurman's alma mater if you please.
Yes. Fine. It's all good. No resentment here.
The boy's welfare is all we've left to consider.

Come June, at the graduation ceremony
wildflowers will dapple the green springtime hill
and after, I'll climb and revisit my old stone chapel.
Maybe then God will have returned, unlocked the doors.
If not, I'll just sit a spell with my gentle friend
the sparrow still cradled in his palm
having survived another harsh winter season
and I'll write my son a poem to recite in celebration
one that sings of perseverance and resolve
the only things that matter truly matter
you just never stop singing—
as the bell tower rings yet another quarter hour.

American Halloween

for Miguel

Like wood-sprites, from house to house
children dart and scamper. Trailing mothers
twist on masks, tug at hems and roll up cuffs
as fathers illuminate flash-lit paths, appealing
"Hold each other's hand. Cross only at the corners!"
I was headed for a grown-up extravaganza
West Hollywood's infamous Halloween parade
when this scene pulled me in. And stopping the car
I sit and observe the great American trick-or-treat tradition.

I had plans to meet a Parisian kitten, "I'll be
waiting for you in pink ears and whiskers"
(she'd have me follow her to France next year).
And certainly her entourage of gay friends would be there
to parade down the boulevard in their *haute couture*
a provocative *fête*, drag queens in outrageous faces
girls as powdered counts, boys, their buxom contessas
a display of fetish in spurious rendition
on this faux fabulous night of exhibition.

But transported by reminiscence, I see my own children
in these young faces—a lion, a knight, and a Disney princess
the high-pitched squeals, collecting treats door to door
their parents on the sidewalk, still lovers
holding hands and waiting their return.
They pass the mean couple's house as my children knew to do
house lights off, those grumpy childless gossips. How they
reveled in another of the neighborhood's juicy divorces

(one more demise of the American dream)
warped and mean, they never gave a thing as I remember
never bought the children's charity chocolate
never gave to save the school's orchestral instruments
not even a few dollars for some holiday paper
to wrap that one gift they splurged on one another.

Ah, but at this house the children will do well.
They seem a fun happy couple, in creepy masks and costumes
carved Jack-o-lanterns on the porch glowing orange
a witch on a broomstick, spiders in webs, their older kids
hidden in the bushes for the ultimate scare.
They remind me of us when we lived here,
before our necks were stretched
pilloried on the judicial block.

The night has grown cold. I've missed the *fête*.
The cat must be mad, wondering, "Does he really care?"
"Did he lose his way?" "Is he for real?" Even if I do arrive
I'll be a son-of-a-bitch for being late, *"putain de merde."*
I won't lie. She'll pout. I'll drive away.

I shift the car in gear and head to the 7-11
for some candy, a frozen dinner and a beer
to sit vigil on the porch with my bag of assorted treats
waiting for the children to arrive, noisy and excited
till they see me sitting in a clown mask with puffy red hair
eating a Hungry Man, alone, on a pumpkin-less porch.

Why Plath Needed a Quality Vault

The reddened rich-wood coffin slid into a packing crate…
legions of bereaved, whisper, console, condole: "At a
time like this, nothing but the best."   Sylvia Plath

I know you Sylvia Plath, as I know elegy in myself.
I too have a suicidal heart beneath my brown chest
having faced the same juries of stodgy literary men
manuscript after manuscript rejected and returned.
Perhaps, like you, not talented enough
nor ambitious enough—so busy raising children and such.
But I'm no Lazarus—I'd get it right the first time through.

So *that* choice I leave for last, under grayer day's overcast
buried beneath the dark weight of myself, no radiance left
no energy to polish my shoes, shave, wash dinner plates
nurse my children back to health, read them stories about
courage and perseverance, on never giving up—as you did
that one frozen night. You taped your babies' door shut
stuffed towels in the cracks so no errant gas could leak in.
It didn't work. They've smelt the fumes their entire lives
the youngest, I understand, following in your wake.

Still, we are bed partners, you and I, on cold winter nights,
lovers I think, rubbing toes together beneath the duvet,
my nightlight illuminating your verse, singing me to sleep.
Like you, I too have studied the *dark and sullen art.*
And though disillusioned, I've yet to seek a quality burial vault
a Wilbert triple-reinforced luxury satin-lined box
strong, so nothing unsavory, like worms, can get in
nor any of my wretched little words leak out.

Sound-sealed for my eternal rest.
Better that way, don't you think?
and like you say, for that—*nothing but the best.*

Then again, I doubt if I'd ever take that escape,
give myself up to the dank earth.
My children keep me too attached, from *flying into black bits.*
Had you considered yours that night—would you have left?
Perhaps you could not resist your disordered mind's need of rest
envied the deep sleep of animals, the odor of overturned earth
sought the same peace you found underneath the house—
(if only for a day and a half) ten years before turning thirty.

Yes, I know you Sylvia Plath
know the verse you shed in life, the pain you fled in death
though never would you guess the ironic result—
a jury of stodgy literary men convened on your behalf
decreed the authenticity of your extraordinary craft
those brilliant pages you left spread across your desk
a quality book at last—your *loving* husband collected into *Ariel.*
You see, dear Sylvia, you finally passed the test—
some goals, I guess, just can't be met in life without a death.
Now on every bookstore shelf PLATH can be found
though they chiseled it as well on a piece of stone.

Hotel Flora, near the Bridge of Sighs

for Christine

Unnerved from sleep by a sudden awakening start—a face
stillborn in ether had passed across my slumbering heart.
Sitting up, I realize where I am—ah yes, my honeymoon again,
Venezia, a 16th century hotel room near the Bridge of Sighs
your beautiful face on the pillow asleep at my side. No ghost.
I've calmed down, though the sentient unease has left its mark
like the trail of a snail across dewy paving stones
having crawled its steady way throughout the night
leaving garden petals with slimy holes.
And leaning against the frame, I recite my mantra again,
"I'm loved now, amen. Don't screw this one up. I'm loved
now, amen. Don't screw this one up. I'm loved now. . . ."

Looking down at the white silk gown lying beside me
an exposed breast, your gorgeous moonlit body softly breathing
already seeded with new life, four months in the making
forty-six chromosomes tucked inside bloody unseen cavities.
And hearing violins, I rise, slowly, so as not to wake you,
go to the open window that I might breathe and relive
the intimate evening spent sitting in St. Marco's square
gazing at you across a table your fragile fingers
feeding me lemon wafers, like hosts, with *Bitter Campari*—
our sweet communion—as violins lifted
Puccini's "Nessun Dorma" into evening air.

But what of the face that startled me out of sleep?
Opening wide the shutters, the pungent odor of Venice canals
ageless mold, gasoline, the death of sunken fish lingers.

Then, a singer's voice lifts from the square, "*Vincero vincero*
vincero" accompanied by the light lap of a gondola passing
delivering fresh catch for tomorrow's *secundo piato*
and from somewhere behind lace curtains
a woman's pleasure is released, or is it a ghost, a lover passed
still haunting these ancient corridors—
for *no one sleeps* tonight I guess.

Suddenly, that face I'd been dreaming all along returns
having left its sentient grief, a sticky trail across my heart
and I whisper, "Father, are you alright?" Closing the shutters
I remember again his puffy eyes at the airport gate
the impression approaching death made on his face
having come to see us off, his damaged liver acting up
deep sacs beneath sallow eyes
the smell of alcohol he could not disguise with Chicklets
the slapping of backs because we're men
his stubborn resistance to my release
pulling me back into his acrid breath
for one final embrace, against the stubble of his chin
the awkward kiss that lingered on my cheek
so desperate to hold his little boy one last time
the one he thought—still didn't know.

As the plane pulled back from the dock
I remember taking your hand for solace
and I knew you that you knew too.
And peering out through the oval glass

I could imagine his face in the crowd
standing vigil at the passenger gate, as was his habit
to insure that I was safe, his chore of love—
the only one he had left now that his children were grown.

And ascending, looking down from three thousand feet
I saw two headlights forging their way across the earth
and imagined his slow trail home
past liquor stores and open bars
along Old Cemetery Road.

In the Time of Frost

for Gabriella

That this late flower should bloom
in the time of frost. Astonishing, her birth
like an *aubade*, a rare blossoming in snowfall
opening up mornings as if to a skyfull of spring
though December's chilly nights bring frigid air
and the cold-leafy scent of winter death.

Morning sounds from the bassinet,
draw me to her faint babbling. I arrive
where she lies warbling and cooing like a pigeon.
Sun rays stream through the window, dissipating cold
and I marvel how the heart can resurrect
filling my hands with love, cradling her against my chest
her warm breath soft against my cheek
wisps of hair the smell of puppies
her knowledge of me confined to what's seen and heard
unaware of age, my slower step, my graying hair.

For me, it would have been a bleak winter season
tucking and oiling my saddle-bags of skin
all the hours wasted in retired hobbies
golf, crossword puzzles, learning Rachmaninoff again.
Just a waste of hands that never held more music
than the bundle I cradle mornings.
Blessed with the first of my day's benedictions
her plum lips cooing at my ear
she brightens my soul's marble mausoleum
wafting the scent of heaven she so recently left.

Experience—my one advantage.
I know more now of fleeting innocence.
Her older siblings, already in commerce
know the irrecusable price of growing up.
On darker days, I think, "What have I done?"
at twenty-one she will see her father old and immobile
unable to carry her across impassable ravines
my cataract eyes, like dirty panes
straining to see her smile
deaf ears reaching for her soothing voice
my stiff hands, like blocks of ice.
All my senses in permanent winter.

My only defense—it was spring. And that season
I'd consumed mouthfuls of her mother's love.
A hungry kiss so reminiscent of teenage lust and desire
brought one last surge of strength that fed the final thrust
like a flame burning brightest at taper's end
sending consequence into every corner of the fertile earth
that this late flower should bloom in the time of frost.

I Forget Me as Son

who could call his father
and ask about life
the pain of growing up
mistakes in love, surviving loss, irreversible regret
how to fix the plumbing of the heart
directions for the road when I thought it time I left
directions home if ever I got lost
or questions about the fear of death—his, of course,
for I was young and too immortal for that.
But in his waning years I'd call to ask
"Tell me father, can you see him coming?"
"Is he in the room?"

And now that I am only father
I forget me as son who could call and inquire
"Is this the right bass for a *Guajira* or *Cuba Son*?"
And patiently he'd beat out the rhythm on the phone
explain the difference between the *Samba* and the *Danzon*.
I'd listen, stupidly writing nothing down,
taking in only what I needed for the job
leaving the rest inside the library of his mind
naïve in believing I could always return—
how generations lose what should never be forgotten.

Yes, now that I am only father, I forget me as a son,
though my own calls me from time to time to inquire
about life, the pain of growing up,
mistakes in love, surviving loss, an irreversible regret

how to fix the plumbing of the heart
directions for the road when it was his time to take off
directions home if he found himself lost
even my scant knowledge of the Cuba *son*
now that he too seeks a musician's life
though not yet the indelicate questions about death.

Though the time will come
when he'll find himself no longer son, only father
and he'll catch himself dialing my number
press end call, sit a moment with the phone and ponder
that he can no longer call and inquire
about life, the pain of growing up,
mistakes in love, surviving loss, an irreversible regret
how to fix the plumbing of the heart, and yes
those indelicate questions about the fear of death.
If he might see him coming—
will he see him in the room?

Veteranos Day Parade

Think of the number sacrificed, proud *mexica* sons
on bloody temple stones, for war, in honor of the gods
those with holes in their chests would know how glory is won

who slung stones at horses, and Spaniards holding arquebus guns
who hung Maximillian, and drove the French from their home
think of the number sacrificed, proud *mexica* sons

whose fathers verified tagged toes for identification
whose mothers embraced precious purple commendations
those with holes in their chests would know how glory is won

those with missing limbs from explosions in desert sand
gurney'd half-bodies splattered in blood-stinking vans
think of the number sacrificed, proud *mexica* sons.

They're marching in east L.A. today for immigration reform
los veteranos of U.S. wars so proud of their service in uniform
those with holes in their chests would know how glory is won

know body bags, the piles on which they are slung
as America denies immigrant soldiers the better life they've earned
think of the number they'll sacrifice next time, proud *mexica* sons
those with holes in their chests will know how glory is won.

Old Weed

> What weed,
> what living waters will give life to us.
>
> Octavio Paz

Tonight, like still life, your body
stretched out across the couch, TV on
a bowl of pistachios, a glass of wine on the coffee table
our infant asleep, dreaming in life's deep wonder
and I think, years from now, she will not sleep like this
her generation's drug of choice will fill her lungs
remove anxiety, depression, make parties more fun
as she discovers, once again, what boys are really after
how lives get governed by one chance encounter
in the hunting and gathering of a mate. But now no matter—
she slumbers in comfort, angel's breath on her cheek.

I step out into the garden to feel the close and covered night
unseasonably cold, strange for California's summer time of year.
A pearl moon, waxing full, tangling itself in the blue plum
like a piece of white fruit hanging from the bough
illuminates a possum shuffling its ugly snout
come to purge the last of this season's harvest.
"So few plums on the branches," you warned.
"Pick what's left. I'll preserve them in Mason jars,"
like your Polish grandmother did back in Wisconsin
when young and resourceful—living on a farm.
But I've been distracted, and let them drop to the ground
smashed now in their splashed and spoiled sadness.
And looking up at a star-filled sky, I wonder, what's out there?
The *immensity of nothing* I suspect.
Such indifference, it feels, to our being here.

I spot my little cherub statue stolen from a cemetery
He's staring at me, my little stone angel on the porch.
He was tossed into a storage bin because of two broken feet.
They'd buried *mi abuelo* there next to his wife months apart.
He'd fled revolution and poverty only to fight prejudice and hate
no privilege in Kansas unless you were white. Nevertheless,
he worked hard painting railroad cars for Atchison Topeka and
Santa Fe, absorbing toxic fumes, low pay with no benefits.
Until his kidneys failed and took him out without a fight.
"Couldn't live without *abuela*," *mis familiares* suspect.

And finding myself in Paz's *labyrinth of solitude*
I enter the tool shed to find some old weed.
Its dry and odorless, old medicine I'd bought—then forgot.
Thought it might work. It didn't.
Life continued spinning out of control, struggling to find work
purpose, the freedom and equality my grandfather sought.
I roll and smoke it anyway, under close and covered night
beneath the blue plum, feeling possums waddling in the dark.
And toking, I see the stone cherub move its cheeks
"realismo magico," my grandfather would have thought.
When a sultry voice reaches me through the screen,
"You coming in?" I can see your PJs unbuttoned at the breasts. "I
poured you a glass. Our favorite movie is about to start."

Naturally, I give that choice a second thought
but the stone cherub from my ancestral grounds
keeps moving his cheeks. This time, I swear, it even winks

But then, the moon becomes eclipsed by a noisy helicopter light.
I kneel with my hands clasped behind my back
smiling in jest, ready to give myself up without a fight
till your quip one-ups my comic relief, "Don't worry.
You're safe. I'll tell them you were with me all night."
Then you wink, "Though I know you'd prefer to write."
She's tolerant that way, patient with my persistent art.
But hearing Bogart's voice on the TV
I think of all I've done to get to this joint
(and all I might never have done
had I smoked too much of this when I was young).
And flipping the blunt against the gnarled trunk
I cross the screen door threshold, lie next to you on the couch
undo the remaining buttons to the waist . . .
as Sam sings Rick's song as if singing just for us.

Waking, I see we've fallen asleep
I hear the baby moving in her crib
the clock ticking on the wall, the TV's steady sign-off hum.
I give her the bottle so you can rest.
But holding our child cozy in my arms
I hear those hungry possums shuffling in the yard
imagine their pointy snouts poking at the plums
the precious ones you wanted to preserve
      but that I, so irresponsibly, left unguarded.

Ladders

We need them to be born—for climbing down
invisible weight, so unwieldy on the ground
we toss them to the side of the road
en route to our new caretakers' home
from the happy hospital maternity ward.

In overgrown brush, weed-lashed
our ladders lie abandoned over the ensuing years—forgotten
through innocence, youth, adolescence and growth
adult failures and triumphs, till the owners, growing old
some wheelchair bound, are unable to sleep
sick to death of ill-health, ready to leave it all behind—
the what-might-have-beens, the dream of life.
They reclaim their ladders from the cloying weeds
lean them against the wall for the inevitable climb.
ready to make the arduous return
escape the walls of this laborious yard.

I left my ladder in Detroit
and for a long time, forgot I'd left one there
My body, young, so lean and strong,
aspirations fought for, some won, life so all-consuming and full
I gave my ladder no thought, lost in grasp and consumption.
Till one night in a fitful dream, my wooden rungs loomed up
to remind me of the climb we all one day will endeavor
and step by step, I looked toward the sky, and at the top
back down to the sacred ground—
my wife gardening, collecting plums

our child tasting the rich blue fruit,
with sloppy hands, face and tongue.

And I could taste them too, a life so sweet
it all seemed permanent somehow
like the soundness of the earth's crust, my writing desk
not just particles and waves in constant flux and motion
but solid and compound—like love and faith and dust.
And I looking down I saw others
leaning their ladders against the wall.
Some, it appeared, had put it off so long
their wooden rungs were perilous with rot
made more dangerous with each passing year.

No matter, I thought, toward freedom I'll escape
stepping off the final rung of my ghostly ladder
en route from the sad hospital to the city morgue
about to step over, I took a step down,
up again, then down, up, down, till merciful heaven—
I awoke in my bed covered in sweat.

Looking at myself in the mirror
a relatively young man
precious blue plums still hanging from the boughs
I wondered at the difficulty to climb that final step—
when it was so easy climbing down.

Blue Plums & Weeds

MARIO RENÉ PADILLA

About the Author

Mario René Padilla was born in Detroit and raised in Columbus, Ohio. He's of Italian and Mexican descent, but grew up, *nevertheless*, a "mid-western" kid. Multi-culturalism and cultural identity are central themes in his work. He is a winner of a Fulbright Award for his dissertation, *Jorge Luis Borges: Young Poet of Prose (1919-1925)*. His first collection of poems, *Reaching Back for the Neverendings,* appeared in 1993. His short stories "Scales" recently won first prize in TulipTree Publishing's story contest, *Stories That Need to Be Told,* 2020. His story "La Château Possonniere" won the prize in 2017. He received a B.S from Ohio State University, an M.A. in English from Loyola Marymount, and a Ph.D. in Comparative Lit. from USC. He's a longtime resident of Venice, CA with his wife and blended family of six. He teaches English, Creative Writing and Latin-American Literature full-time at Santa Monica College in Santa Monica, California.

PSPOETS

Los Angeles, CA